M000074887

Treasury of French Love Poems

VOLUME 2

Bilingual Love Poems

Treasury of French Love Poems

VOLUME 2

IN FRENCH AND ENGLISH

EDITED BY

Lisa Neal

HIPPOCRENE BOOKS, INC.
New York

Grateful acknowledgment is made to Editions Gallimard for permission
to reprint "L'amoureuse" from *Capitale de la douleur* by Paul Éluard,
copyright © 1926; "Barbara" from *Paroles* by Jacques Prévert,
copyright © 1949; "A★★★" in "A une sérénité crispée" from
Recherche de la base et du sommet by René Char, copyright © 1955;
"Aube" from *Airs* by Philippe Jaccottet, copyright © 1967.

Copyright © 2003 Hippocrene Books.

All rights reserved.

Book design and composition by Susan A. Ahlquist, East Hampton, NY.

For more information, address:
HIPPOCRENE BOOKS, INC.
171 Madison Avenue
New York, NY 10016

ISBN 0-7818-0930-4

Cataloging-in-Publication Data available from the Library of Congress.

Printed in the United States of America.

Table of Contents

Poems

MARIE DE FRANCE (Thirteenth Century)

Chevrefoil

Assez me plest e bien le voil
Del lai que hum nume *Chevrefoil*
Que la verité vus en cunte
E pur quei il fut fet e dunt.
Plusurs le m'unt cunté e dit
E jeo l'ai trové en escrit
De Tristram e de la reine,
De lur amur qui tant fu fine,
Dunt il eurent meinte dolur,
Puis en mururent en un jur.

Li reis Marks esteit curucié
Vers Tristram sun nevuz irié ;
De sa tere le cungëasss
Pur la reïne qu'il ama.
En sa cuntree en est alez ;
En Suhtwales, u il fu nez,
Un an demurat tut entier,
Ne pot ariere repeirier;
Mes puis se mist en abandun
De mort e de destructiun.

MARIE DE FRANCE (Thirteenth Century)

Goatleaf (Honeysuckle)

It pleases me to tell you
The truth about why
The lay called *Honeysuckle*
Was made, and about whom.
Many told and recounted it
To me, and I found it written,
About Tristram and the queen
About their love so fine
That caused them to suffer
And to die on the same day.

King Marc was angry
With Tristram his nephew;
Exiled him from his land
For the sake of the queen
He loved. To his own country
Tristram went, South Wales,
Where he was born,
Remained a whole year there,
Could not return, but then began
To court death and destruction.

Ne vus esmerveillez neent :
Kar ki eime mut lëalement,
Mut est dolenz e trepensez
Quant il nen ad ses volentez.
Tristram est dolent et pensis ;
Pur ceo s'esmut de sun païs.
En Cornouaille vait tut dreit,
La u la reïne maneit
En la forest tut sul se mist,
Ne voleit pas que hum le veïst ;
En la veprée s'en eisseit,
Quant tens de herberger esteit ;
Od païsanz, od povre gent
Preneit la nuit herbergement.
Les noveles lur enquereit
Del rei cum il se cunteneit.
Ceo li dient qu'il unt oï
Que li barun erent bani,
A Tintagel deivent venir :
Li reis i veolt sa curt tenir ;
A Pentecuste i serunt tuit,
Mut i avra joie e deduit,
E la reïne i sera.
Tristram l'oï, mut se haïta :
Ele ne purat mie aller
K'il ne la veie trespasser.

Do not be astonished; for
Anyone who loves truly
Is pained and very sad
When deprived of his desire.
Tristram was pained and sad:
And so he left his land
And straight to Cornwall went,
Where the queen was staying.
Into the forest he went alone,
Wanted no one to see him there,
Came out at eventide,
When it was time for shelter;
With peasants or the poor
He spent the night.
He asked them news
Of the king, what he did.
They said they'd heard
The barons had been called
To Tintagel, where the king
Was to hold his court;
They'd all be there at Pentecost,
For pleasure and delight,
And the queen with them.
Tristram heard this with joy:
She could not pass without
Him seeing her go by.

Le jur que li rei fu meüz,
Tristram est al bois revenuz.
Sur le chemin que il saveit
Que la rute passer deveit,
Une codre trencha par mi,
Tute quarreie la fendi.
Quand il ad paré le bastun,
De sun cutel escrit sun nun :
Se la reïne s'aperceit,
Qui mut grant garde en preneit
— Autre feit li fu avenu
Que si l'aveit aparceü —
De sun ami bien conuistra
Le bastun, quant el le verra.
Ceo fut la summe de l'escrit
Qu'il li aveit mandé e dit :
Que lunges ot ilec esté
E atendu e surjurné
Pur espïer e pur saver
Coment il la peüst veer,
Kar ne pot nent vivre sanz li ;
D'euls deux fu il tut autresi
Cume del chevrefoil esteit
Ki a la codre se perneit :
Quant il s'i est laciez e pris
E tut entur le fust s'est mis,
Ensemble poënt bien durer ;

The day the king set out
Tristram came to the wood
Along the path he knew
They must travel;
He cut and trimmed a hazel,
And when he'd made a stick,
Carved his name along its flank.
If the queen caught sight of it,
She'd mark it mighty well —
He'd done the same before
And she had seen it —
She'd recognize the stick
As belonging to her lover.
This was what he'd written,
What he'd conveyed and said:
That he had long been here
And waited and remained
To watch and to find out
How he could see her,
For he couldn't live without her,
They were like the honeysuckle
That winds around the beech:
When it has laced and twined
And gone all round the trunk,
They can live together a long time;

Mes ki puis les volt desevrer,
Li codres muert hastivement
E li chevrefoil ensement.
"Bele ami, si est de nus :
Ne vus sanz mei, ne mei sanz vus !"

La reïne vait chevachant ;
Elle esgardat tut un pendant,
Le bastun vit, bien l'aparceut,
Tutes les lettres i conut.
Les chevalers que la menoënt,
Quë ensemblë od li erroënt,
Cumanda tuz a arester :
Descendre vot e resposer.
Cil unt fait sun commandement.
Ele s'en vet luinz de sa gent ;
Sa meschine apelat a sei,
Brenguein, que fu de bone fei.
Del chemin un poi s'esluina ;
Dedenz le bois celui trova
Que plus l'amot que rien vivant
Entre eus meinent joie mut grant.
A li parlat tut a leisir,
E ele li dit sun pleisir ;
Puis li mustre cumfatement

But if you try to separate them,
The beech soon dies
And the honeysuckle too.
"Dear friend, so it is with us:
Not you without me, nor I without you!"

The queen was riding along,
She looked up at a slope,
Saw the stick, knew it well,
Recognized all the letters.
The knights accompanying her,
Who rode at her side,
She commanded all to stop:
She wanted to dismount and rest.
They did as she commanded.
She moved away from them,
Called her maid to her side,
The faithful servant Brenguein.
She left the path and in the wood
She found the one she loved
More than anything alive.
There was great joy between them.
He spoke to her at leisure,
She told him all she liked;
Then she explained how

Del rei avrait acordemẹnt,
E que mut li aveit pesé
De ceo qu'il l'ot si cungïé ;
Par encusement l'aveit fait.
Atant s'en part, sun ami lait ;
Mes quant ceo vient al desevrer,
Dunc commencerent a plurer.
Tristram a Wales s'en rala,
Tant que sis uncles le manda.

Pur la joie qu'il ot eüe
De s'amie qu'il ot veüe
E pur ceo k'il aveit escrit,
Si cum la reïne l'ot dit,
Pur les paroles remembrer,
Tristram, ki bien saveit harper,
En aveit feit un nuvel lai ;
Asez briefment le numerai :
Gotelef l'apelent en anglais,
Chevrefoil le nument Franceis.
Dit vus en ai la verité
Del lai que j'ai ici cunté.

He would be reconciled
With the king, who had
Exiled him, to her dismay,
Because of accusations.
Then she left her lover;
But when they parted,
They began to weep.
Tristram went back to Wales,
To await his uncle's summons.

Because he'd had such joy
On seeing his beloved,
and because he'd written
As the queen had told him,
To remember the words
Tristram, harping sweetly,
Had made a new lay;
I shall name it briefly:
Goatleaf it's called in English
Chevrefeuille in French.
Now I've told you the truth
About the lay I've sung.

(TRANSLATED BY LISA NEAL)

ALAIN CHARTIER (1386–1449)

de *"La Belle Dame Sans Mercy"*

Disner fut prest et tables mises.
Les dames à table s'assirent
Et, quand elles furent assises,
Les plus gracieux les servirent.
Telz y ot qui, à ce jour, virent
En la compaignie layens
Leurs juges, dont semblant ne firent,
Qui les tiennent en leurs lyens.

Un entre les autres y vy
Qui souvent aloit et venoit
Et pensoit comme homme ravy
Et gaires de bruit ne menoit.
Son semblant tresfort contenoit,
Mais desir passoit la raison
Qui souvent son regart menoit
Tel fois qui n'estoit pas saison.

ALAIN CHARTIER (1386–1449)

From *"The Beautiful Merciless Lady"*

The bordes were spred in right little space,
The ladies sat each as hem[1] seemed best,
There were no deadly servants in the place,
But chosen men, right of the goodliest:
And some there were, peraventure most freshest,
That saw their judges full demure,
Without semblaunt, either to most or lest,
Notwithstanding they had hem under cure.

Emong all other, one I gan espy,
Which in great thought ful often came and went,
As one that had been ravished utterly:
In his language not greatly dilligent,
His countenance he kept with great turment,
But his desire farre passed his reason,
For ever his eye went after his entent,
Full many a time, whan it was no season.

---

1. Them.

De faire chiere s'efforçoit
Et menoit une joie fainte
Et à chanter son cuer forsoit
Non pas pour plaisir, mais pour crainte.
Car tousjours ung relais de plainte
S'enlaçoit au son de sa voix
Et revenoit à son attainte
Comme l'oisel au chant du boys.

Des autres y ot pleine salle,
Mais cellui trop bien me sembloit
Ennuyé, mesgre, blesme et palle,
Et la parolle lui trembloit.
Gaires aux autres n'assembloit :
Le noir portoit (et sans devise !)
Et trop bien homme resembloit
Qui n'a pas son cuer en franchise.

De toutes festoier faignoit :
Bien le fist et bien lui seoit.
Mais, à la fois, le contraignoit
Amours qui son cuer ardeoit
Pour sa maistresse qu'il veoit,
Que je choisi lors clerement
A son regart qu'il asseoit
Sur elle si piteusement.

To make chere sore himselfe he pained,
And outwardly he fained great gladnesse,
To sing also by force he was constrained,
For no pleasaunce, but very shamefastnesse:
For the complaint of his most heavinesse
Came to his voice, alway without request,
Like as the soune of birdes doth expresse,
Whan they sing loud in frithe or in forrest.

Other there were that served in the hall
But none like him, as after mine advise,[2]
For he was pale, and somwhat lean withall,
His speech also trembled in fearful wise,
And ever alone, but whan he did servise,
All blacke he ware, and no devise but plain:
Me thought by him, as my wit could suffise,
His herte was nothing in his own demain.[3]

To feast hem all he did his dilligence,
And well he coud, right as it seemed me,
But evermore, whan he was in presence,
His chere was done, it nolde[4] none other be:
His schoolemaister had such aucthorite,
That, all the while he bode still in the place,
Speake coud he not, but upon her beautie
He looked still with a right pitous face.

2. Observation.
3. Control.
4. For *ne wold*, would not.

Assez sa face destornoit
Pour regarder en autres lieux,
Mais au travers l'œil retornoit
Au lieu qui lui plaisoit le mieulx.
J'apperçeu le trait de ses yeulx
Tout empenné d'humbles requestes,
Et dis à par moy : "Si m'ait Dieux,
Autel fusmes comme vous estes !"

A la fois à part se tiroit
Pour raffermer sa contenance
Et trestendrement souppiroit
Par douloureuse souvenance.
Puis reprenoit son ordonnance
Et venoit pour servir les mes,
Mais, à bien jugier sa semblance,
C'estoit ung piteux entremes.

Aprez disner on s'avança
De danser, chascun et chascune.
Et le triste amoureux dansa
Adez o l'autre, adez o l'une.
A toutes fist chiere commune.
O chacune à son tour aloit.
Mais tousjours revenoit à une
Dont sur toutes plus lui chaloit.

With that his head he tourned at the last
For to behold the ladies everichone,[5]
But ever in one he set his eye stedfast
On her which his thought was most upon,
For of his eyen the shot[6] I knew anone;
Which fearful was, with right humble requests:
Than to my self I said, by God alone,
Such one was I, or that I saw these jests.

Out of the prease he went full easely
To make stable his heavie countenance,
And wote ye well, he sighed wonderly
For his sorrowes and wofull remembrance:
Than in himselfe he made his ordinance,
And forthwithall came to bring in the messe,
But for to judge his most wofull pennance,
God wote it was a pitous entremesse.[7]

After dinner anon they hem avanced
To daunce above the folke everichone,
And forthwithall, this heavy man he daunced,
Somtime with twain and somtime with one:
Unto hem all his chere was after one,
Now here, now there, as fell by aventure,
But ever among he drew to her alone
Which he most dread of living creature.

5. Every one.
6. Glance.
7. "Entremet," a dish served between the courses.

Bien à mon gré fust advisé,
Entre celles que je vy lors
S'il eust au gré du cuer visé
Autant qu'à la beauté du corps.
Qui croit de legier les rapports
De ses yeulx, sans autre esperance,
Pourroit mourir de mille mors
Avant qu'attaindre à sa plaisance.

En la dame ne failloit riens,
Ne plus avant ne plus arriere.
C'estoit garnison de tous biens
Pour faire à cuer d'amant frontiere :
Jeune, gente, fresche et entiere,
Maintien rassis et sans changier,
Doulce parolle et grant maniere
Dessoubz l'estandart de Dangier.

De celle feste me lassay,
Car joie triste cuer traveille ;
Et hors de la presce passay
Et m'assis derriere une treille
Drue de fueilles à merveille,
Entrelacee de saulx vers,
Si que nul, pour l'espesse fueille,
Ne me povoit veoir à travers.

To mine advise good was his purveiance,[8]
Whan he her chose to his maistresse alone,
If that her herte were set to his pleasance,
As much as was her beauteous person:
For who so ever setteth his trust upon
The report of the eyen, withouten more,
He might be dead, and graven under stone,
Or ever he should his hertes ease restore.

In her failed nothing that I coud gesse,
One wise nor other, privie nor apert,[9]
A garrison she was of all goodlinesse,
To make a frontier for a lovers herte:
Right yong and fresh, a woman full covert,
Assured wele of port, and eke of chere,
Wele at her ease withouten wo or smert,
All underneath the standerd of dangere.

To see the feast it wearied me full sore,
For heavy joy doth sore the herte travaile:
Out of the prease I me withdrow therefore,
And set me downe alone behind a traile,[10]
Full of leaves, to see a great mervaile,
With greene wreaths ybounden wonderly,
The leaves were so thicke withouten faile,
That throughout no man might me espy.

---

8. Foresight.
9. Secret nor public.
10. Trellis

L'amoureux sa dame menoit
Danser, quant venoit à son tour,
Et puis seoir s'en revenoit
Sur ung preau vert, au retour.
Nulz autres n'avoit alentour
Assis, fors seulement les deux,
Et n'y avoit autre destour
Fors la treille entre moy et eulx.

J'oy l'amant qui soupiroit,
Car qui plus est prez, plus desire,
Et la grant douleur qu'il tiroit
Ne savoit taire et n'osoit dire :
Si languissoit auprez du mire
Et nuisoit à sa garison :
Car qui art ne se peut plus nuire
Qu'aprocher le feu du tyson.

Le cuer en son corps lui croissoit
D'angoisse et de paour estraint,
Tant qu'à bien peu qu'il ne froissoit
Quant l'un et l'autre le contraint :
Desir boute, crainte refraint.
L'ung eslargit, l'autre reserre.
Si n'a pas peu de mal empraint
Qui porte en son cuer telle guerre.

To this lady he came full courtesly,
Whan he thought time to dance with her a trace,[11]
Set in an herber,[12] made full pleasantly,
They rested hem fro thens but a little space:
Nigh hem were none of a certain compace,[13]
But onely they, as farre as I coud see:
Save the traile, there I had chose my place,
There was no more between hem two and me.

I heard the lover sighing wonder sore,
For aye the more the sorer it him sought,
His inward paine he coud not keepe in store,
Nor for to speake so hardie was he nought,
His leech was nere, the greater was his thoght,
He mused sore to conquer his desire:
For no man may to more pennance be broght
Than in his heat to bring him to the fire.

The herte began to swell within his chest,
So sore strained for anguish and for paine,
That all to peeces almost it to brest,
Whan both at ones so sore it did constraine,
Desire was bold, but shame it gan refraine,
That one was large, the other was full close:
No little charge was laid on him, certaine,
To keepe such werre, and have so many fose.

---

11. A turn or measure.
12. Arbor.
13. Compass, circle, distance.

De parler souvent s'efforça,
Se crainte ne l'eust destorné.
Mais en la fin son cuer força
Quant il ot assez sejourné.
Puis s'est vers la dame torné
Et dist bas en plorant adonques :
"Mal jour fut pour moy ajourné,
Ma dame, quant je vous vy onques".

Full oftentimes to speak himself he pained,
But shamefastnesse and drede said ever nay,
Yet at the last, so sore he was constrained,
Whan he full long had put it in delay,
To his lady right thus than gan he say,
With dredeful voice, weeping, half in a rage:
"For me was purveyed an unhappy day,
When I first had a sight of your visage!"

(TRANSLATED BY GEOFFREY CHAUCER)

FRANÇOIS VILLON (1431–1489)

Les regrets de la belle Heaulmière
(La Vielle en regrettant le temps de sa jeunesse)

Advis m'est que j'oy regreter
La belle qui fut hëaulmiere,
Soy jeune fille soushaitter
Et parler en telle maniere:
"Ha ! Vieillesse felonne et fiere,
Pourquoi m'as si tost abatue ?
Qui me tient, qui, que ne me fiere,
Et qu'a ce coup je ne me tue ?

Tollu m'as la haulte franchise
Que beaulté m'avoit ordonné
Sur clers, marchans et gens d'Esglise :
Car lors il n'estoit homme né
Qui tout le sien ne m'eust donné,
Quoy qu'il en fust des repentailles,
Mais que luy eusse habandonné
Ce que reffusent truandailles.

FRANÇOIS VILLON (1431–1489)

The Complaint of the Fair Armoress

Meseemeth I heard cry and groan
That sweet who was the armourer's maid;
For her young years she made sore moan,
And right upon this wise she said;
"Ah fierce old age with foul bald head,
To spoil fair things thou art over fain,
Who holdeth me? who? would God I were dead!
Would God I were well dead and slain!

"Lo, thou hast broken the sweet yoke
That my high beauty held above
All priests and clerks and merchant-folk;
Here was not one but for my love
Would give me gold and gold enough,
Though sorrow his very heart had riven,
To win from me such wage thereof
As now no thief would take if given.

A maint homme l'ay reffusé,
Quin'estoit a moy grant sagesse,
Pour l'amour d'ung garson rusé,
Auquel j'en feiz grande largesse.
A qui que je feisse finesse,
Par m'ame, je l'amoye bien !
Or ne me faisoit que rudesse,
Et ne m'amoit que pour le mien.

Si ne me sceut tant detrayner,
Fouler aux piez, que ne l'aymasse,
Et m'eust il fait les rains trayner,
S'il m'eust dit que je le baisasse,
Que tous mes maulx je n'oubliasse.
Le glouton, de mal entechié,
M'embrassoit . . . J'en suis bien plus grasse !
Que m'en reste il ? Honte et pechié.

Or est il mort, passé trente ans,
Et je remains, vielle, chenue.
Quant je pense, lasse ! au bon temps,
Quelle fus, quelle devenue !
Quant me regarde toute nue,

Et je me voy si tres changiee,
Povre, seiche, megre, menue,
Je suis presque toute enragiee.

"I was right chary of the same,
God wot it was my great folly,
For love of one sly knave of them,
Good store of that same sweet had he;
For all my subtle wiles, perdie,
God wot I loved him well enow;
Right evilly handled me
But he loved well my gold, I trow.

"Though I gat bruises green and black,
I loved him never the less a jot;
Though he bound burdens on my back,
If he said, 'Kiss me, and heed it not,'
Right little pain I felt, God wot,
When that foul thief's mouth, found so sweet,
Kissed me — Much good thereof I got!
I keep the sin and the shame of it.

"And he died thirty year agone.
I am Old now, no sweet thing to see;
By God, though, when I think thereon,
And of that good glad time, woe's me,
And stare upon my changed body

Stark naked, that has been so sweet,
Lean, wizen, like a small dry tree,
I am nigh mad with the pain of it.

Qu'est devenu ce front poly,
Cheveulx blons, ces sourcils voultiz,
Grant entroeil, ce regart joly,
Dont prenoie les plus soubtilz ;
Ce beau nez droit, grant ne petiz,
Ces petites jonctes oreilles,
Menton fourchu, cler vis traictiz,
Et ces belles levres vermeilles ?

Ces gentes espaulles menues,
Ces bras longs et ces mains traictisses,
Petiz tetins, hanches charnues,
Eslevees, propres, faictisses
A tenir amoureuses lisses ;
Ces larges rains, ce sadinet
Assis sur grosses fermes cuisses,
Dedens son petit jardinet ?

Le front ridé, les cheveux gris,
Les sourcilz cheus, les yeulx estains,
Qui faisoient regars et ris
Dont mains marchans furent attains ;
Nez courbes de beaulté loingtains,
Oreilles pendantes, moussues,
Le vis pally, mort et destains,
Menton froncé, levres peaussues :

"Where is my faultless forehead's white
The lifted eyebrows, soft gold hair,
Eyes wide apart and keen of sight,
With subtle skill in the amorous air;
The straight nose, great nor small, but fair,
The small carved ears of shapeliest growth,
Chin dimpling, color good to wear,
And sweet red splendid kissing mouth!

"The shapely slender shoulders small,
Long arms, hands wrought in glorious wise,
Round little breasts, the hips withal
High, full of flesh, not scant of size,
Fit for all amorous masteries;
(. . .)[1]

"A wrinkled forehead, hair gone gray,
Fallen eyebrows, eyes gone blind and red,
Their laughs and looks all fled away,
Yea, all that smote men's hearts are fled;
The bowed nose, fallen from goodlihead;
Foul flapping ears like water-flags;
Peaked chin, and cheeks all waste and dead,
And lips that are two skinny rags:

---

1. Expurgated lines:
   Those broad loins, and that charming thing
   Set in plump firm thighs
   Within its little garden?

C'est d'umaine beauté l'issue !
Les bras cours et les mains contraites,
Les espaulles toutes bossues ;
Mamelles, quoy ? Toutes retraites ;
Telles les hanches que les tetés ;
Du sadinet, fy ! Quant des cuisses,
Cuisses ne sont plus, mais cuissetes
Grivelees comme saulcisses.

Ainsi le bon temps regretons
Entre nous, povres vielles sotes
Assises bas, a crouppetons,
Tout en ung tas comme pelotes,
A petit feu de chenevotes
Tost allumees, tost estaintes ;
Et jadis fusmes si mignotes ! . . .
Ainsi en prent a mains et maintes".

"Thus endeth all the beauty of us.
The arms made short, the hands made lean,
The shoulders bowed and ruinous,
The breasts, alack! all fallen in
The flanks too, like the breasts, grown thin;
(. . .)²
For the lank thighs, no thighs but skin,
They are specked with spots like sausage-meat.

"So we make moan for the old sweet days,
Poor old light women, two or three
Squatting above the straw-fire's blaze,
The bosom crushed against the knee,
Like fagots on a heap we be,
Round fires soon lit, soon quenched and done;
And we were once so sweet, even wel
Thus fareth many and many an one."

(TRANSLATED BY A. C. SWINBURNE)

---

2. Expurgated line:
   That charming thing? Horrors!

FRANÇOIS VILLON (1431–1489)

Ballade des femmes de Paris

Quoiqu'on tient belles langagères
Florentines, Vénitiennes,
Assez pour être messagères,
Et mêmement les anciennes,
Mais soient Lombardes, Romaines.
Genevoises, à mes périls,
Pimontoises, savoisiennes,
Il n'est bon bec que de Paris.

De beau parler tiennent chaïères,
Ce dit-on, les Napolitaines,
Et sont très bonnes caquetiéres
Allemandes et Prussiennes ;
Soient Grecques, Egyptiennes,
De Hongrie ou d'autres pays,
Espagnoles ou Catelennes,
Il n'est bon bec que de Paris.

Brettes, Suisses n'y savent guères,
Gasconnes, n'aussi Toulousaines :
De Petit Pont deux harengères

FRANÇOIS VILLON (1431–1489)

The Ballad of the Women of Paris

Albeit the Venice girls get praise
For their sweet speech and tender air,
And though the old women have wise ways
Of chaffering for amorous ware,
Yet at my peril dare I swear,
Search Rome, where God's grace mainly tarries,
Florence and Savoy, everywhere,
There's no good girl's lip out of Paris.

The Naples women, as folk prattle,
Are sweetly spoken and subtle enough:
German girls are good at tattle,
And Prussians make their boast thereof —
Take Egypt for the next remove,
Or that waste land the Tartar harries,
Spain or Greece, for the matter of lose,
There's no good girl's lip out of Paris.

Breton and Swiss know nought of the matter,
Gascony girls or girls of Toulouse;
Two fishwomen with a half-hour's chatter

Les concluront, et les Lorraines,
Angloises et Calaisiennes,
(Ai-je beaucoup de lieux compris ?)
Picardes de Valenciennes ;
Il n'est bon bec que de Paris.

Prince, aux dames parisiennes
De bien parler donnez le prix ;
Quoi que l'on die d'Italiennes,
Il n'est bon bec que de Paris

Would shut them up by threes and twos;
Calais, Lorraine, and all their crews,
(Names enow the mad song marries)
England and Picardy, search them and choose,
There's no good girl's lip out of Paris.

Prince, give praise to our French ladies
For the sweet sound their speaking carries;
'Twixt Rome and Cadiz many a maid is
But no good girl's lip out of Paris.

(Translated by A. C. Swinburne)

JACQUES TAHUREAU (1527–1555)

En quel fleuve areneux jaunement s'écouloit

En quel fleuve areneux jaunement s'écouloit
L'or, qui blondist si bien les cheveux de ma dame ?
Et du brillant esclat de sa jumelle flamme,
Tout astre surpassant, quel haut ciel s'emperloit ?

Mais quelle riche mer le coral receloit
De cette belle levre, où mon desir s'affame ?
Mais en quel beau jardin, la rose qui donne ame
A ce teint vermeillet, au matin s'estaloit ?

Quel blanc rocher de Pare, en etofe marbrine
A tant bien montagné ceste plaine divine ?
Quel parfum de Sabée a produit son odeur ?

O trop heureux le fleuve, heureux ciel, mer heureuse,
Le jardin, le rocher, la Sabée odoreuse,
Qui nous ont enlustré le beau de son honneur !

JACQUES TAHUREAU (1527–1555)

Shadows of His Lady

Within the sand of what far river lies
The gold that gleams in tresses of my Love?
What highest circle of the Heavens above
Is jeweled with such stars as are her eyes?

And where is the rich sea whose coral vies
With her red lips, that cannot kiss enough?
What dawn-lit garden knew the rose, whereof
The fled soul lives in her cheeks' rosy guise?

What Parian marble that is loveliest,
Can make the whiteness of her brow and breast?
When drew she breath from the Sabæn glade?

Oh, happy rock and river, sky and sea,
Gardens and glades Sabæn, all that be
The far-off splendid semblance of my maid.

(Translated by Andrew Lang)

PIERRE DE RONSARD (1524–1586)

Je vous envoie un bouquet . . .

Je vous envoie un bouquet que main
Vient de trier de ces fleurs épanies ;
Qui ne les eût à ce vêpre cueillies,
Chutes à terre elles fussent demain.

Cela vous soit un exemple certain
Que vos beautés, bien qu'elles soient fleuries,
En peu de temps cherront, toutes flétries,
Et, comme fleurs, périront tout soudain.

Le temps s'en va, le temps s'en va, ma Dame
Las ! Le temps, non, mais nous nous en allons,
Et tôt serons étendus sous la lame ;

Et des amours desquelles nous parlons,
Quand serons morts, n'en sera plus nouvelle.
Pour c'aimez-moi cependant qu'êtes belle

PIERRE DE RONSARD (1524–1586)

Roses

I send you here a wreath of blossoms blown,
And woven flowers at sunset gathered,
Another dawn had seen them ruined, and shed
Loose leaves upon the grass at random strown.

By this, their sure example, be it known,
That all your beauties, now in perfect flower,
Shall fade as these, and wither in an hour,
Flowerlike, and brief of days, as the flower sown.

Ah, time is flying, lady, time is flying;
Nay, 'tis not time that flies but we that go,
Who in short space shall be in churchyard lying,

And of our loving parley none shall know,
Nor any man consider what we were;
Be therefore kind, my love, whilst thou art fair.

(TRANSLATED BY ANDREW LANG)

PIERRE DE RONSARD (1524–1586)

Ode à sa maîtresse

Mignonne, allons voir si la rose,
Qui ce matin avait déclose
Sa robe de pourpre au soleil,
A point perdu cette vêprée
Les plis de sa robe pourprée
Et son teint au vôtre pareil.

Las ! Voyez comme en peu d'espace,
Mignonne, elle a dessus la place,
Las ! Las ! Ses beautés laissé choir !
Ô vraiment marâtre Nature,
Puisqu'une telle fleur ne dure
Que du matin jusques au soir !

Donc si vous me croyez, mignonne,
Tandis que votre âge fleuronne
En sa plus verte nouveauté,
Cueillez, cueillez votre jeunesse.
Comme à cette fleur la vieillesse
Fera ternir votre beauté.

PIERRE DE RONSARD (1524–1586)

The Rose

See, Mignonne, hath not the Rose,
That this morning did unclose
Her purple mantle to the light,
Lost before the day be dead,
The glory of her raiment red,
Her color, bright as yours is bright?

Ah, Mignonne, in how few hours
The petals of her purple flowers
All have faded, fallen, died;
Sad Nature, mother ruinous,
That seest thy fair child perish thus
'Twixt matin song and even-tide
Hear me, my darling, speaking sooth,
Gather the fleet flower of your youth,
Take ye your pleasure at the best;
Be merry ere your beauty flit,
For length of days will tarnish it
Like roses that were loveliest.

(TRANSLATED BY ANDREW LANG)

PIERRE DE RONSARD (1524–1586)

Fleur Angevine de quinze ans . . .

Fleur Angevine de quinze ans,
Ton front monstre assez de simplesse,
Mais ton cœur ne cache au dedans
Sinon que malice et finesse,
Celant sous ombre d'amitié
Une jeunette mauvaistié.

Ren moy, si tu as quelque honte,
Mon cœur que je t'avois donné,
Don't tu ne fais non-plus de conte
Que d'un esclave emprisonné,
T'esjouïssant de sa misere,
Et te plaisant de luy desplaire.

Une autre moins belle que toy,
Mais de bien meilleure nature,
Le voudroit bien avoir de moy.
Elle l'aura, je te le jure ;
Elle l'aura, puis qu'autrement
Il n'a de toy bon traitement.

Mais non : j'aime trop mieux qu'il meure
Sans esperance en ta prison,
J'aime trop mieux qu'il y demeure
Mort de douleur contre raison,
Qu'en te changeant jouïr de celle
Qui m'est plus douce, et non si belle.

PIERRE DE RONSARD (1524–1586)

To His Young Mistress

Fair flower of fifteen springs, that still
Art scarcely blossomed from the bud,
Yet hast such store of evil will,
A heart so full of hardihood,
Seeking to hide in friendly wise
The mischief of your mocking eyes.

If you have pity, child, give o'er,
Give back the heart, you stole from me,
Pirate, setting so little store
On this your captive from Love's sea,
Holding his misery for gain,
And making pleasure of his pain.

Another, not so fair of face,
But far more pitiful than you,
Would take my heart, if of his grace,
My heart would give her of Love's due;
And she shall have it, since I find
That you are cruel and unkind.

Nay, I would rather that I died,
Within your white hands prisoning,
Would rather that it still abide
In your ungentle comforting,
Than change its faith, and seek to her
That is more kind, but not so fair.

(Translated by Andrew Lang)

LOUISE LABÉ (1526–1566)

Élégie VIII

Tout aussi tot que je commence à prendre
      Dens le mol lit le repos desiré,
      Mon triste esprit hors de moy retiré,
      S'en va vers toy incontinent se rendre.
Lors m'est avis que dedens mon sein tendre
      Je tiens le bien, où j'ay tant aspiré,
      Et pour lequel j'ay si haut souspiré
      Que de sanglots ay souvent cuidé fendre.
O dous sommeil, o nuit à moy heureuse !
      Plaisant repos plein de tranquilité,
      Continuez toutes les nuiz mon songe :
Et si jamais ma povre ame amoureuse
      Ne doit avoir de bien en verité,
      Faites au moins qu'elle en ait en mensonge.

LOUISE LABÉ (1526–1566)

Povre âme amoureuse (Sapphics)

When to my lone soft bed at eve returning
Sweet desir'd sleep already stealeth o'er me,
My spirit flieth to the fairy-land of her tyrannous love.
Him then I think fondly to kiss, to hold him
Frankly then to my bosom; I that all day
Have looked for him suffering, repining, yea many long days.
O bless'd sleep, with flatteries beguile me;
So, if I ne'er may of a surety have him,
Grant to my poor soul amorous the dark gift of this illusion.

(TRANSLATED BY ROBERT BRIDGES)

LOUISE LABÉ (1526–1566)

Tant que mes yeux . . .

Tant que mes yeux pourront larmes épandre
A l'heur passé avec toi regretter,
Et qu'aux sanglots et soupirs résister
Pourra ma voix, et un peu faire entendre ;

Tant que ma main pourra les cordes tendre
Du mignard luth, pour tes grâces chanter ;
Tant que l'esprit se voudra contenter
De ne vouloir rien fors que toi comprendre,

Je ne souhaite encore point mourir.
Mais, quand mes yeux je sentirai tarir,
Ma voix cassée, et ma main impuissante,

Et mon esprit en ce mortel séjour
Ne pouvant plus montrer signe d'amante,
Prierai la mort noircir mon plus clair jour.

LOUISE LABÉ (1526–1566)

Long As I Still Can Shed Tears

Long as I still can shed tears from mine eyes
My bliss with thee regretting once again,
And while my voice, though in a weaker strain,
Can speak a little, checking sobs and sighs;

Long as my hand can tune the harmonies
Of my bold lute to sing thy grace fain;
And while my spirit shall content remain,
Thee understanding, nothing else to prize,

So long I do not yet desire to die;
But when I feel mine eyes are growing dry,
Broken my voice, my hand devoid of skill,

My spirit in this its dwelling-place of clay
Able no more to shew I love thee still,
I shall pray Death to blot my clearest day.

(TRANSLATED BY ARTHUR PLATT)

ANTOINE DE CHANDIEU (1534–?, Swiss)

Qu'as-tu ? pauvre amoureux . . .

Qu'as-tu ? pauvre amoureux, dont l'âme demi morte
Soupire des sanglots au vent qui les emporte.
N'accuse rien que toi. Ton mal est ton désir,
Et ce dont tu te plains, est ton propre plaisir.
Tu n'as autre repos que ce qui te tourmente,
Et t'éjouis au mal dont tu vas soupirant,
Buvant ce doux-amer qui t'enivre et qui rend
Ton plaisir douloureux et ta douleur plaisante.

ANTOINE DE CHANDIEU (1534–?, Swiss)

What is wrong? Poor lover . . .

What is wrong? Poor lover whose soul, half dead,
Sighs sobs into the wind that carries them away.
Accuse only yourself. Your unhappiness is your desire.
Your lament is the very source of your pleasure.
You have no rest but that which torments you.
You take pleasure in a sickness for which you yearn,
You drink in the bitter-sweet that inebriates, making
Your pleasure painful and your pain pleasurable.

(Translated by Lisa Neal)

PHILIP DESPORTES (1545–1606)

Quand nous aurons passé l'Infernale rivière

Quand nous aurons passé l'Infernale rivière,
Vous & moy pour nos maux damnez aux plus bas lieux,
Moy pour avoir sans cesse idolâtré vos yeux
Vous pour être à grand tort de mon cœur la meurtrière.

Si je puis toujours voir votre belle lumière,
Les éternelles nuits, les regrets furieux
N'étonneront mon âme, et l'Enfer odieux
N'aura point de douleur qui me puisse être fière.

Vous pourrez bien aussi vos tourments modérer,
Avec le doux plaisir de me voir endurer,
Si lors vous vous plaisez encor en mes traverses.

Mais puis que nous avons failli diversement,
Vous par inimitié, moy par trop vous aimant,
J'ay peur qu'on nous sépare en deux chambres diverses.

PHILIP DESPORTES (1545–1606)

Sonnet

When, you and I, we shall have passed th' infernal stream,
Damn'd, for our several sins, unto the deeps of hell,
I for idolatry, that loved your eyes o'er well,
You, for my heart you slew with cruelty extreme,

If your fair eyes I see forever on me beam,
Neither the eternal night nor pine unquenchable
My courage shall confound nor all the pains that dwell
In those infernal deeps shall cruel to me seem.

You, too, if pleasure yet you take in your disdains
And in my miseries, still may moderate your pains
With watching me endure the torments of my doom.

But, since, on divers ways, we in this world above
Sinned, you for sheer despite and I for too much love,
I fear they'll sunder us, each in a several room.

(TRANSLATED BY JOHN PAYNE)

JEAN DE LA FONTAINE (1621–1695)

L'Amour et la Folie

Tout est mystère dans l'Amour,
Ses flèches, son Carquois, son Flambeau, son Enfance.
Ce n'est pas l'ouvrage d'un jour
Que d'épuiser cette Science.
Je ne prétends donc point tout expliquer ici.
Mon but est seulement de dire, à ma manière,
Comment l'Aveugle que voici
(C'est un Dieu), comment, dis-je, il perdit la lumière ;
Quelle suite eut ce mal, qui peut-être est un bien ;
J'en fais juge un Amant, et ne décide rien.

La Folie et l'Amour jouaient un jour ensemble.
Celui-ci n'était pas encor privé des yeux.
Une dispute vint : l'Amour veut qu'on assemble
Là-dessus le Conseil des Dieux.
L'autre n'eut pas la patience ;
Elle lui donne un coup si furieux,
Qu'il en perd la clarté des Cieux.

JEAN DE LA FONTAINE (1621–1695)

Love and Folly

Love's worshippers alone can know
The thousand mysteries that are his;
His blazing torch, his twanging bow,
His blooming age are mysteries.
A charming science — but the day
Were all too short to con it o'er;
So take of me this little lay,
A sample of its boundless lore.

As once, beneath the fragrant shade
Of myrtles fresh in heaven's pure air,
The children, Love and Folly, played
A quarrel rose betwixt the pair.
Love said the gods should do him right —
But Folly vowed to do it then,
And struck him, o'er the orbs of sight,
So hard he never saw again.

Vénus en demande vengeance.
Femme et mère, il suffit pour juger de ses cris :
Les Dieux en furent étourdis,
Et Jupiter, et Némésis,
Et les Juges d'Enfer, enfin toute la bande.
Elle représenta l'énormité du cas.
Son fils, sans un bâton, ne pouvait faire un pas :
Nulle peine n'était pour ce crime assez grande.
Le dommage devait être aussi réparé.
Quand on eut bien considéré
L'intérêt du Public, celui de la Partie,
Le résultat enfin de la suprême Cour
Fut de condamner la Folie
A servir de guide à l'Amour.

His lovely mother's grief was deep,
She called for vengeance on the deed;
A beauty does not vainly weep,
Nor coldly does a mother plead.
A shade came o'er the eternal bliss
That fills the dwellers of the skies;
Even stony-hearted Nemesis
And Rhadamanthus wiped their eyes.
"Behold," she said, "this lovely boy,"
While streamed afresh her graceful tears —
"Immortal, yet shut out from joy
And sunshine, all his future years.
The child can never take, you see,
A single step without a staff —
The hardest punishment would be
Too lenient for the crime by half."

All said that Love had suffered wrong,
And well that wrong should be repaid;
Then weighed the public interest long,
And long the party's interest weighed.
And thus decreed the court above:
"Since Love is blind from Folly's blow,
Let Folly be the guide of Love,
Where'er the boy may choose to go."

(Translated by W. C. Bryant)

VICTOR HUGO (1802–1885)

Puisque j'ai mis ma lèvre à ta coupe encor pleine . . .

Puisque j'ai mis ma lèvre à ta coupe encor pleine ;
Puisque j'ai dans tes mains posé mon front pâli ;
Puisque j'ai respiré parfois la douce haleine
De ton âme, parfum dans l'ombre enseveli ;

Puisqu'il me fut donné de t'entendre me dire
Les mots où se répand le cœur mystérieux ;
Puisque j'ai vu pleurer, puisque j'ai vu sourire
Ta bouche sur ma bouche et tes yeux sur mes yeux ;

Puisque j'ai vu briller sur ma tête ravie
Un rayon de ton astre, hélas ! voilé toujours ;
Puisque j'ai vu tomber dans l'onde de ma vie
Une feuille de rose arrachée à tes jours ;

Je puis maintenant dire aux rapides années :
— Passez ! passez toujours ! je n'ai plus à vieillir !
Allez-vous-en avec vos fleurs toutes fanées ;
J'ai dans l'âme une fleur que nul ne peut cueillir !

Votre aile en le heurtant ne fera rien répandre
Du vase où je m'abreuve et que j'ai bien rempli.
Mon âme a plus de feu que vous n'avez de cendre !
Mon cœur a plus d'amour que vous n'avez d'oubli !

VICTOR HUGO (1802–1885)

More Strong than Time

Since I have set my lips to your full cup, my sweet,
Since I my pallid face between your hands have laid,
Since I have known your soul, and all the bloom of it,
And all the perfume rare, now buried in the shade;

Since it was given to me to hear one happy while,
The words wherein your heart spoke all its mysteries,
Since I have seen you weep, and since I have seen you smile,
Your lips upon my lips, and your eyes upon my eyes;

Since I have known above my forehead glance and gleam,
A ray, a single ray, of your star, veiled always,
Since I have felt the fall, upon my lifetime's stream,
Of one rose petal plucked from the roses of your days;

I now am bold to say to the swift changing hours,
Pass, pass upon your way, for I grow never old,
Fleet to the dark abysm with all your fading flowers,
One rose that none may pluck, within my heart I hold.

Your flying wings may smite, but they can never spill
The cup fulfilled of love, from which my lips are wet;
My heart has far more fire than you can frost to chill,
My soul more love than you can make my soul forget.

(TRANSLATED BY ANDREW LANG)

VICTOR HUGO (1802–1885)

À une femme

Enfant ! si j'étais roi, je donnerais l'empire,
Et mon char, et mon sceptre, et mon peuple à genoux
Et ma couronne d'or, et mes bains de porphyre,
Et mes flottes, à qui la mer ne peut suffire,

Pour un regard de vous !

Si j'étais Dieu, la terre et l'air avec les ondes,
Les anges, les démons courbés devant ma loi,
Et le profond chaos aux entrailles fécondes,
L'éternité, l'espace, et les cieux, et les mondes,

Pour un baiser de toi !

VICTOR HUGO (1802–1885)

To a Woman

Child! if I were a king, my throne I would surrender,
My scepter, and my chariot, and kneeling vavassours,
My golden crown, and porphyry baths, and consorts tender,
And fleets that fill the seas, and regal pomp and splendor,

    All for one look of yours!

If I were God, the earth and luminous deeps that span it,
Angels and demons bowed beneath my word divine,
Chaos profound, with flanks of flaming gold and granite,
Eternity, and space, and sky, and sun, and planet,

    All for one kiss of thine.

(TRANSLATED BY W. J. ROBERTSON)

ALFRED DE MUSSET (1810–1857)

Tristesse

J'ai perdu ma force et ma vie,
Et mes amis et ma gaieté ;
J'ai perdu jusqu'à la fierté
Qui faisait croire à mon génie.

Quand j'ai connu la Vérité,
J'ai cru que c'était une amie ;
Quand je l'ai comprise et sentie,
J'en étais déjà dégoûté.

Et pourtant elle est éternelle,
Et ceux qui se sont passés d'elle
Ici-bas ont tout ignoré.

Dieu parle, il faut qu'on lui réponde.
Le seul bien qui me reste au monde
Est d'avoir quelquefois pleuré.

ALFRED DE MUSSET (1810–1857)

Tristesse

Lost is my strength, my mirth, the joy intense
Of very life, the comrades and the zest;
All even to my pride, that unsuppressed
Had wrought my spirit to self-confidence.

When truth I recognized, my raptured sense
Dreamed I had found a love to be caressed;
But palling as I clasped her to my breast
Loathing and ashes were my recompense.

Yet is she still divine; and they that curled
The lip in sight of her have dulled their ears
To wisdom's echoes in our under-world.

God speaks: perforce my naked soul replies;
One thing of all is left me, that mine eyes
Have sometimes been not unacquaint with tears.

(TRANSLATED BY JAMES ROBERTSON)

THÉOPHILE GAUTIER (1811–1872)

Coquetterie posthume

Quand je mourrai, que l'on me mette,
Avant de clouer mon cercueil,
Un peu de rouge à la pommette,
Un peu de noir au bord de l'œil.

Car je veux dans ma bière close,
Comme le soir de son aveu,
Rester éternellement rose
Avec du khôl sous mon œil bleu.

Pas de suaire en toile fine,
Mais drapez-moi clans les plis blancs
De ma robe de mousseline,
De ma robe à treize volants.

C'est ma parure préférée ;
Je la portais quand je lui plus.
Son premier regard l'a sacrée,
Et depuis je ne la mis plus.

THÉOPHILE GAUTIER (1811–1872)

Posthumous Coquetry

Let there be laid, when I am dead,
Ere 'neath the coffin-lid I lie,
Upon my cheek a little red,
A little black about the eye.

For I in my close bier would fain,
As on the night his vows were made,
Rose-red eternally remain,
With kohl beneath my blue eye laid.

Wind me no shroud of linen down
My body to my feet, but fold
The white folds of my muslin gown
With thirteen flounces as of old.

This shall go with me where I go:
I wore it when I won his heart;
His first look hallowed it, and so,
For him, I laid the gown apart.

Posez–moi, sans jaune immortelle,
Sans coussin de larmes brodé,
Sur mon oreiller de dentelle
De ma chevelure inondé.

Cet oreiller, dans les nuits folles,
A vu dormir nos fronts unis,
Et sous le drap noir des gondoles
Compté nos baisers infinis.

Entre mes mains de cire pâle,
Que la prière réunit,
Tournez ce chapelet d'opale,
Par le pape à Rome bénit :

Je l'égrènerai dans la couche
D'où nul encor ne s'est levé ;
Sa bouche en a dit sur ma bouche
Chaque Pater et chaque Ave.

 64

No immortelles, no broidered grace
Of tears upon my cushions be;
Lay me on my pillow's lace,
My hair across it like a sea.

That pillow, those mad nights of old,
Has seen our slumbering brows unite,
And 'neath the gondola's black fold
Has counted kisses infinite.

Between my hands of ivory,
Together set for prayer and rest,
Place then the opal rosary
The holy Pope at Rome has blest

I will lie down then on that bed
And sleep the sleep that shall not cease;
His mouth upon my mouth has said
Pater and *Ave* for my peace.

(TRANSLATED BY ARTHUR SYMONS)

CHARLES BAUDELAIRE (1821–1867)

La géante

Du temps que la Nature en sa verve puissante
Concevait chaque jour des enfants monstrueux,
J'eusse aimé vivre auprès d'une jeune géante,
Comme aux pieds d'une reine un chat voluptueux.

J'eusse aimé voir son corps fleurir avec son âme
Et grandir librement de ses terribles jeux ;
Deviner si son cœur couve une sombre flamme
Aux humides brouillards qui nagent dans ses yeux ;

Parcourir à loisir ses magnifiques formes ;
Ramper sur le versant de ses genoux énormes,
Et parfois en été, quand les soleils malsains,

Lasse, la font s'étendre à travers la campagne,
Dormir nonchalamment à l'ombre de ses seins,
Comme un hameau paisible au pied d'une montagne.

CHARLES BAUDELAIRE (1821–1867)

Giantess

When Nature once in lustful hot undress
Conceived gargantuan offspring, then would I
Have loved to live near a young giantess,
Like a voluptuous cat at a queen's feet.

To see her body flower with her desire
And freely spread out in its dreadful play
Guess if her heart concealed some heavy fire
Whose humid smokes would swim upon her eye.

To feel at leisure her stupendous shapes,
Crawl on the cliffs of her enormous knees,
And, when in summer the unhealthy suns

Have stretched her out across the plains, fatigued,
Sleep in the shadows of her breasts at ease
Like a small hamlet at a mountain's base.

(TRANSLATED BY KARL J. SHAPIRO)

CHARLES BAUDELAIRE (1821–1867)

Allégorie

C'est une femme belle et de riche encolure,
Qui laisse dans son vin traîner sa chevelure.
Les griffes de l'amour, les poisons du tripot,
Tout glisse et tout s'émousse au granit de sa peau.
Elle rit à la mort et nargue la Débauche,
Ces monstres dont la main, qui toujours gratte et fauche,
Dans ses jeux destructeurs a pourtant respecté
De ce corps ferme et droit la rude majesté.
Elle marche en déesse et repose en sultane ;
Elle a dans le plaisir la foi mahométane,
Et dans ses bras ouverts, que remplissent ses seins,
Elle appelle des yeux la race des humains.
Elle croit, elle sait, cette vierge inféconde
Et pourtant nécessaire à la marche du monde,
Que la beauté du corps est un sublime don
Qui de toute infamie arrache le pardon.
Elle ignore l'Enfer comme le Purgatoire,
Et quand l'heure viendra d'entrer dans la Nuit noire,
Elle regardera la face de la Mort,
Ainsi qu'un nouveau-né, — sans haine et sans remord.

CHARLES BAUDELAIRE (1821–1867)

An Allegory

Here is a woman, richly and fair,
Who in her wine dips her long, heavy hair;
Love's claws, and that sharp poison which is sin,
Are dulled against the granite of her skin.
Death she defies, Debauch she smiles upon,
For their sharp scythe-like talons every one
Pass by her in their all-destructive play;
Leaving her beauty till a later day.
Goddess she walks; sultana in her leisure;
She has Mohammed's faith that heaven is pleasure,
And bids all men forget the world's alarms
Upon her breast, between her open arms.
She knows, and she believes, this sterile maid,
Without whom the world's onward dream would fade,
That bodily beauty is the supreme gift
Which may from every sin the terror lift.
Hell she ignores, and Purgatory defies;
And when black Night shall roll before her eyes,
She will look straight in Death's grim face forlorn,
Without remorse or hate — as one new-born.

(TRANSLATED BY F. P. STURM)

CHARLES BAUDELAIRE (1821–1867)

La beauté

Je suis belle, ô mortels ! comme un rêve de pierre,
Et mon sein, où chacun s'est meurtri tour à tour,
Est fait pour inspirer au poète un amour
Éternel et muet ainsi que la matière.

Je trône dans l'azur comme un sphinx incompris ;
J'unis un cœur de neige à la blancheur des cygnes ;
Je hais le mouvement qui déplace les lignes
Et jamais je ne pleure et jamais je ne ris.

Les poètes, devant mes grandes attitudes,
Que j'ai l'air d'emprunter aux plus fiers monuments,
Consumeront leurs jours en d'austères études ;

Car j'ai, pour fasciner ces dociles amants,
De purs miroirs qui font toutes choses plus belles :
Mes yeux, mes larges yeux aux clartés éternelles !

CHARLES BAUDELAIRE (1821–1867)

Beauty

I am as lovely as a dream in stone,
And this my heart where each finds death in turn,
Inspires the poet with a love as lone
As clay eternal and as taciturn.

Swan-white of heart, a sphinx no mortal knows,
My throne is in the heaven's azure deep;
I hate all movements that disturb my pose,
I smile not ever, neither do I weep.

Before my monumental attitudes
That breathe a soul into the plastic arts
My poets pray in austere studious moods,

For I, to fold enchantment round their hearts,
Have pools of light where beauty flames and dies,
The placid mirrors of my luminous eyes.

(TRANSLATED BY F. P. STURM)

RENÉ SULLY PRUDHOMME (1839–1907)

Prière

Ah ! Si vous saviez comme on pleure
De vivre seul et sans foyers,
Quelquefois devant ma demeure
Vous passeriez.

Si vous saviez ce que fait naître
Dans l'âme triste un pur regard,
Vous regarderiez ma fenêtre
Comme au hasard.

Si vous saviez quel baume apporte
Au cœur la présence d'un cœur,
Vous vous assoiriez sous ma porte
Comme une sœur.

Si vous saviez que je vous aime,
Surtout si vous saviez comment,
Vous entreriez peut-être même.

RENÉ SULLY PRUDHOMME (1839–1907)

A Supplication

Oh! did you know how the tears apace
Fall by a lonely heart, alas!
I think that before my dwelling place

Sometimes you did pass.

And did you know of the hopes that arise
In wearied soul from a pure young glance,
Maybe to my window you'd lift your eyes

As if by chance.

And if of the comfort you only knew
A heart may bring to a heart that is sore
You'd rest a while, as a sister may do,

Beside my door.

But if you knew of the love that enwraps
My soul for you, and holds it fast,
Quite simple over my threshold, perhaps,

You'd step at last.

(TRANSLATED BY I. O. L.)

PAUL VERLAINE (1844–1896)

Tiré de *Romances Sans Paroles : IV*

O triste était mon âme . . .
O triste, triste était mon âme
A cause, à cause d'une femme.

Je ne me suis pas consolé
Bien que mon cœur s'en soit allé,

Bien que mon cœur, bien que mon âme
Eussent fui loin de cette femme.

Je ne me suis pas consolé,
Bien que mon cœur s'en soit allé.

Et mon cœur, mon cœur trop sensible
Dit à mon âme : Est-il possible,

Est-il possible, - le fût-il,
Ce fier exil, ce triste exil ?

Mon âme dit à mon cœur : Sais-je,
Moi-même, que nous veut ce piège

D'être présents bien qu'exilés
Encore que loin en allés ?

PAUL VERLAINE (1844–1896)

From *Romances Sans Paroles: IV*

O sad, sad was my soul, alas!
For a woman! a woman's sake it was.

I have had no comfort since that day,
Although my heart went its way,

Although my heart and soul went
From the woman into banishment.

I have had no comfort since that day,
Although my heart went its way.

And my heart, being sore in me,
Said to my soul: How can this be?

How can this be or have been thus,
This proud, sad banishment of us?

My soul said to my heart: Do I
Know what snare we are tangled by,

Seeing that, banished, we know not whether
We are divided or together?

(TRANSLATED BY ARTHUR SYMONS)

PAUL VERLAINE (1844–1896)

Tiré de *Romances Sans Paroles : VII*

Les roses étaient toutes rouges
Et les lierres étaient tout noirs.

Chère, pour peu que tu ne bouges,
Renaissent tous mes désespoirs.

Le ciel était trop bleu, trop tendre,
La mer trop verte et l'air trop doux.

Je crains toujours, – ce qu'est d'attendre !
Quelque fuite atroce de vous.

Du houx à la feuille vernie
Et du luisant buis je suis las,

Et de la campagne infinie
Et de tout, fors de vous, hélas !

PAUL VERLAINE (1844–1896)

From *Romances Sans Paroles: VII*

The roses were all red,
The ivy was all black:
Dear, if you turn your head,
All my despairs come back.

The sky was too blue, too kind,
The sea too green, and the air
Too calm; and I know in my mind
I shall wake and not find you there.

I am tired of the box-tree's shine
And the holly's that never will pass,
And the plain's unending line,
And all but you, alas.

(Translated by Arthur Symons)

ARTHUR RIMBAUD (1854–1891)

Sensation

Par les soirs bleus d'été, j'irai dans les sentiers,
Picoté par les blés, fouler l'herbe menue :
Rêveur, j'en sentirai la fraîcheur à mes pieds.
Je laisserai le vent baigner ma tête nue.

Je ne parlerai pas, je ne penserai rien,
Mais l'amour infini me montera dans l'âme ;
Et j'irai loin, bien loin, comme un bohémien,
Par la Nature, heureux- comme avec une femme.

ARTHUR RIMBAUD (1854–1891)

Sensation

On summer evenings blue, pricked by the wheat
On rustic paths the thin grass I shall tread,
And feel its freshness underneath my feet,
And, dreaming, let the wind bathe my bare head.

I shall not speak, nor think, but, walking slow
Through Nature, I shall rove with Love my guide,
As gypsies wander, where, they do not know,
Happy as one walks by a woman's side.

(TRANSLATED BY JETHRO BITHELL)

ÉMILE VERHAEREN (1855–1916, Belgian)

Dans la maison où notre amour a voulu naître

Dans la maison où notre amour a voulu naître,
Avec les meubles chers peuplant l'ombre et les coins,
Où nous vivons à deux, ayant pour seuls témoins
Les roses qui nous regardent par les fenêtres.

Il est des jours choisis, d'un si doux réconfort,
Et des heures d'été, si belles de silence,
Que j'arrête parfois le temps qui se balance,
Dans l'horloge de chêne, avec son disque d'or.

Alors l'heure, le jour, la nuit est si bien nôtre
Que le bonheur qui nous frôle n'entend plus rien,
Sinon les battements de ton cœur et du mien
Qu'une étreinte soudaine approche l'un de l'autre.

ÉMILE VERHAEREN (1855–1916, Belgian)

In the House Where our Love was Born

In the house where our love was born,
Surrounded by good furniture filling shadows and corners,
Where we lived, just the two of us, having as our only witnesses
The roses watching us through the windows.

These are precious days of such sweet comfort,
And summer moments so beautifully silent,
That I sometimes stop the time that swings
In the oak grandfather clock with the gold pendulum.

Then time — the day, the night — is so much ours
That the happiness touching us hears nothing more
Except the beating of your heart and mine
That a sudden embrace brings close together.

(TRANSLATED BY LISA NEAL)

ALBERT SAMAIN (1858–1900)

Nuit blanche

Cette nuit, tu prendras soin que dans chaque vase
Frissonne, humide encore, une gerbe de fleurs.
Nul flambeau dans la chambre - où tes chères pâleurs
Se noieront comme un rêve en des vapeurs de gaze.

Pour respirer tous nos bonheurs avec emphase,
Sur le piano triste, où trembleront des pleurs,
Tes mains feront chanter d'angéliques douleurs
Et je t'écouterai, silencieux d'extase.

Tels nous nous aimerons, sévères et muets.
Seul, un baiser parfois sur tes ongles fluets
Sera la goutte d'eau qui déborde des urnes,

O Sœur ! et dans le ciel de notre pureté
Le virginal Désir des amours taciturnes
Montera lentement comme un astre argenté.

ALBERT SAMAIN (1858–1900)

Sleepless Night

Tonight there shall be lighted here no tapers,
But a sheaf of still wet flowers that shake in frailness
Shall light thy chamber — where thy tender paleness
Shall like a dream be drowned in white gauze vapors.

That we may breathe a bliss without alloy,
On the sad piano where the flowers shake
Play thou a song of angels' hearts that ache,
And I shall swoon into a tranced joy.

So we will love, mute and austere. Save this,
That sometimes on thy slender hand a kiss
Shall be the drop that overflows the urn.

Sister! And in the skies that o'er us bend
The chaste desire of passion taciturn
Shall slowly like a silver star ascend.

(TRANSLATED BY JETHRO BITHELL)

MARIE NIZET (1859–1922, Belgian)

La bouche

Ni sa pensée, en vol vers moi par tant de lieues,
Ni le rayon qui court sur son front de lumière,
Ni sa beauté de jeune dieu qui la première
Me tenta, ni ses yeux - ces deux caresses bleues ;

Ni son cou ni ses bras, ni rien de ce qu'on touche,
Ni rien de ce qu'on voit de lui ne vaut sa bouche
Où l'on meurt de plaisir et qui s'acharne à mordre,

Sa bouche de fraîcheur, de délices, de flamme,
Fleur de volupté, de luxure et de désordre,
Qui vous vide le cœur et vous boit jusqu'à l'âme . . .

MARIE NIZET (1859–1922, Belgian)

The Mouth

Not his thought, on flight toward me over such a distance,
Nor the wrinkle that runs across his radiant forehead,
Nor his Greek-God beauty that was the first
To tempt me, nor his eyes — those two blue kisses;

Not his neck, nor arms nor anything you can touch,
Not anything of him you see is worth his mouth
Where one dies of pleasure and which tries desperately to bite,

His fresh, delectable, flaming mouth,
Flower of voluptuousness, lust and disorder,
That empties your heart and drinks you up to your very soul . . .

(TRANSLATED BY LISA NEAL)

Pour le livre d'amour

Je puis mourir demain et je n'ai pas aimé.
Mes lèvres n'ont jamais touché lèvres de femme,
Nulle ne m'a donné dans un regard son âme,
Nulle ne m'a tenu contre son cœur pâmé.

Je n'ai fait que souffrir, pour toute la nature,
Pour les êtres, le vent, les fleurs, le firmament,
Souffrir par tous mes nerfs, minutieusement
Souffrir de n'avoir pas d'âme encore assez pure.

J'ai craché sur l'amour et j'ai tué la chair !
Fou d'orgueil, je me suis roidi contre la vie !
Et seul sur cette Terre à l'Instinct asservie
Je défiais l'Instinct avec un rire amer.

Partout, dans les salons, au théâtre, à l'église,
Devant ces hommes froids, les plus grands, les plus fins,
Et ces femmes aux yeux doux, jaloux ou hautains
Dont on redoraient chastement l'âme exquise,

Je songeais : tous en sont venus là ! J'entendais
Les râles de l'immonde accouplement des brutes !
Tant de fanges pour un accès de trois minutes !
Hommes, soyez corrects ! ô femmes, minaudez !

JULES LAFORGUE (1860–1887)

For the Book of Love

I may be dead tomorrow, uncaressed.
My lips have never touched a woman's none
Has given me in a look her soul, not one
Has ever held me swooning at her breast.

I have but suffered, for all nature, trees
Whipped by the winds, wan flowers, the ashen sky,
Suffered with all my nerves, minutely, I
Have suffered for my soul's impurities.

And I have spat on love, and, mad with pride,
Slaughtered my flesh, and life's revenge I brave,
And, while the whole world else was Instinct's slave,
With bitter laughter Instinct I denied.

In drawing-rooms, the theater, the church,
Before cold men, the greatest, most refined,
And women with eyes jealous, proud, or kind,
Whose tender souls no lust would seem to smirch,

I thought: This is the end for which they work!
Beasts coupling with the groaning beasts they capture
And all this dirt for just three minutes' rapture!
Men, be correct! And women, purr and smirk!

(TRANSLATED BY JETHRO BITHELL)

JULES LAFORGUE (1860–1887)

Derniers poèmes, XII

Noire bise, averse glapissante,
Et fleuve noir, et maisons closes,
Et quartiers sinistres comme des Morgues,
Et l'Attardé qui à la remorque traîne
Toute la misère du cœur et des choses,
Et la souillure des innocentes qui traînent,
Et crie à l'averse. « Oh, arrose, arrose
« Mon cœur si brûlant, ma chair si intéressante !»

Oh, elle, mon cœur et ma chair, que fait-elle ? . . .

Oh ! si elle est dehors par ce vilain temps,
De quelles histoires trop humaines rentre-t-elle ?
Et si elle est dedans,
À ne pas pouvoir dormir par ce grand vent,
Pense-t-elle au Bonheur,
Au bonheur à tout prix
Disant: tout plutôt que mon cœur reste ainsi incompris ?
Soigne-toi, soigne-toi! pauvre cœur aux abois.

(Langueurs, débilité, palpitations, larmes,
Oh, cette misère de vouloir être notre femme !)

JULES LAFORGUE (1860–1887)

Last Poems, XII

Black north wind, shrieking rain,
Black river, and locked-up houses,
Neighborhoods sinister like Morgues,
People out late always dragging
All the aches of their heart and things,
And the stains of innocents who
Call to the rain: "Soak, soak
My ardant heart, my oh-so-interesting flesh!"

She, my heart and flesh, what is she doing?

If she's out on the street in this villainous weather
From what too-human histories will she return?
And if she's inside,
Sleepless because of this strong wind,
Is she thinking of Pleasure?
Of pleasure at any price?
Saying: "Anything rather than my heart remaining misunderstood!"
Take care, take care, poor hounded heart.

(Boredom, debility, nervous twitch, tears,
the misery of wanting to be our wife!)

Ô pays, ô famille !
Et l'âme toute tournée
D'héroïques destinées
Au delà des saintes vieilles filles,
Et pour cette année !

Nuit noire, maisons closes, grand vent,
Oh, dans un couvent, dans un couvent !

Un couvent dans ma ville natale
Douce de vingt-mille âmes à peine,
Entre le lycée et la préfecture
Et vis-à-vis la cathédrale,
Avec ces anonymes en robes grises,
Dans la prière, le ménage, les travaux de couture ;
Et que cela suffise . . .
Et méprise sans envie
Tout ce qui n'est pas cette vie de Vestale
Provinciale,
Et marche à jamais glacée,
Les yeux baissés.
Oh ! je ne puis voir ta petite scène fatale à vif,
Et ton pauvre air dans ce huis-clos,
Et tes tristes petits gestes instinctifs,
Et peut-être incapable de sanglots !

Homeland, family,
And the soul turned to
Heroic destinies
The beyond of the old maid saints.
And for this year!

Black night, locked houses, hard wind,
get thee to a convent, to a convent!

The convent in my birthplace
(Hardly twenty thousand souls)
Between the high school and town hall,
In full view of the cathedral
With the anonymous in gray robes
In prayer, housework, sewing
And that suffices —
Despising without desire
All that isn't Provincially Vestal in this life,
Every step glacial.
Eyes downcast.
No! I can't see you in this fatal scene,
Your poor appearance in this cloister
Your little instinctive gestures
Perhaps unable even to sob!

Oh ! ce ne fut pas et ce ne peut être,
Oh ! tu n'es pas comme les autres,
Crispées aux rideaux de leur fenêtre
Devant le soleil couchant qui dans son sang se vautre !
Oh ! tu n'as pas l'âge,
Oh, dis, tu n'auras jamais l'âge,
Oh, tu me promets de rester sage comme une image ? . . .

La nuit est à jamais noire,
Le vent est grandement triste,
Tout dit la vieille histoire
Qu'il faut être deux au coin du feu,
Tout bâcle un hymne fataliste,
Mais toi, il ne faut pas que tu t'abandonnes,
À ces vilains jeux ! . . .
À ces grandes pitiés du mois de novembre !
Reste dans ta petite chambre,
Passe, à jamais glacée,
Tes beaux yeux irréconciliablement baissés.

Oh, qu'elle est là-bas, que la nuit est noire !
Que la vie est une étourdissante foire !
Que toutes sont créature, et que tout est routine !
Oh, que nous mourrons !

Oh, this was not and cannot be
You aren't like the others, all
Stiff at their windows
Facing a sinking sun that wallows in one's blood.
No, you aren't of age,
Tell me you'll never be of age,
Promise me to stay as good as gold . . .

The night is ever black,
The wind hugely sad,
Both tell the same old story
That before the fireplace it takes two
Everyone races through that fateful verse
But you, you can't let yourself be taken in by these games. . . .
These great pities of November!
Stay in your small room
Walk by
Your fine eyes unmelted and irreconcilably cast down.

Oh, she's there and the night is so black!
Life is a dazzling fair
Where all turns to routine.
We will die!

Eh bien, pour aimer ce qu'il y a d'histoires
Derrière ces beaux yeux d'orpheline héroïne,
Ô Nature, donne-moi la force et le courage
De me croire en âge,
Ô Nature relève-moi le front !
Puisque, tôt ou tard, nous mourrons. . . .

And so that I can love the stories behind those beautiful,
heroic orphan eyes
Oh Nature, give me the strength and courage
To believe myself of age
To hold my head high;
For sooner or later, we'll die.

(Translated by Lisa Neal)

VICTOR SÉGALEN (1878–1919)

Éloge de la Jeune Fille

Magistrats ! dévouez aux épouses vos arcs triomphaux.
Enjambez les routes avec la louange des veuves obstinées. Usez
du ciment, du faux marbre et de la boue séchée pour dresser
les mérites de ces dames respectables, — c'est votre emploi.

Je garde le mien qui est d'offrir à une autre un léger tribut de
paroles, une arche de buée dans les yeux, un palais trouble
dansant au son du cœur de la mer.

Ceci est réservé à la seule Jeune Fille. À celle à qui tous les maris
du monde sont promis, — mais qui n'en tient pas encore.

À celle dont les cheveux libres tombent en arrière, sans
empois, sans fidélité, — et les sourcils ont l'odeur de la mousse.

À celle qui a des seins et qui n'allaite pas ; un cœur et n'aime pas ;
un ventre pour les fécondités, mais décemment demeure stérile.

À celle riche de tout ce qui viendra ; qui va tout choisir, tout
recevoir, tout enfanter peut-être.

À celle qui, prête à donner ses lèvres à la tasse des épousailles,
tremble un peu, ne sait que dire, consent à boire, — et n'a pas
encore bu.

VICTOR SÉGALEN (1878–1919)

In Praise of the Young Woman

Politicians! Make your arches of triumph in honor of wives.
Publish far and wide the praise of obstinate widows. Use
cement, imitation marble and even mud to erect monuments
to the virtues of these respectable women. It's your job.

My job is to offer another woman an airy verbal tribute, a
misty arch in the eyes, a shimmering palace dancing to the
sound of the sea's heartbeat.

This is reserved for the Young Woman alone. For the woman
who can choose any husband in the world, but who doesn't
have one quite yet.

For the woman whose hair falls loosely down her back,
without starch or fidelity, whose eyebrows smell like moss.

For the woman who has breasts that don't nurse; a heart that
doesn't love; a womb for fertility that remains decently sterile.

For the woman rich in possibilities; who will choose all,
receive all, maybe even give birth to all.

For the woman who, ready to give her lips to the wedding
cup, trembles a little, knows not what to say, agrees to drink —
but hasn't yet drunk.

(TRANSLATED BY LISA NEAL)

GUILLAUME APOLLINAIRE (1880–1918)

Le Pont Mirabeau

Sous le pont Mirabeau coule la Seine
    Et nos amours
Faut-il qu'il m'en souvienne
La joie venait toujours après la peine

      Vienne la nuit sonne l'heure
      Les jours s'en vont je demeure

Les mains dans les mains restons face à face
    Tandis que sous
Le pont de nos bras passe
Des éternels regards l'onde si lasse

      Vienne la nuit sonne l'heure
      Les jours s'en vont je demeure

L'amour s'en va comme cette eau courante
    L'amour s'en va
Comme la vie est lente
Et comme l'Espérance est violente

      Vienne la nuit sonne l'heure
      Les jours s'en vont je demeure

Mirabeau Bridge

Under the Mirabeau Bridge flows the Seine
And our love
Must I remember
Joy always followed pain

Bells toll in the night
Days go by I remain

Hand in hand let us stay face to face
While underneath the bridge of our arms goes
The tired wave of our ceaseless gaze

Bells toll in the night
Days go by I remain

Love leaves like this flowing water
Love leaves
Oh how slow life is
And how violent Hope

Bells toll in the night
Days go by I remain

Passent les jours et passent les semaines
  Ni temps passé
Ni les amours reviennent
Sous le pont Mirabeau coule la Seine

   Vienne la nuit sonne l'heure
   Les jours s'en vont je demeure

The days go by the weeks go by
　　　　Neither time past
　　Nor love return
Under the Mirabeau Bridge flows the Seine

　　　　Bells toll in the night
　　　　Days go by I remain.

(TRANSLATED BY LISA NEAL)

PAUL ÉLUARD (1895–1952)

L'amoureuse

Elle est debout sur mes paupières
Et ses cheveux sont dans les miens,
Elle a la forme de mes mains,
Elle a la couleur de mes yeux,
Elle s'engloutit dans mon ombre
Comme une pierre sur le ciel.

Elle a toujours les yeux ouverts
Et ne me laisse pas dormir.
Ses rêves en pleine lumière
Font s'évaporer les soleils,
Me font rire, pleurer et rire,
Parler sans avoir rien à dire.

From *Capitale de la douleur* by Paul Éluard, © Editions Gallimard, 1926.

PAUL ÉLUARD (1895–1952)

The Lover

She is standing on my eyelids,
Her hair in mine,
She has taken the shape of my hands
And the color of my eyes
She is swallowed by my shadow
Like a rock by the sky.

Eyes ever open
She does not let me sleep.
Her daydreams
Make suns evaporate
And make me laugh, cry and laugh,
Speak with nothing to say.

(TRANSLATED BY LISA NEAL)

Barbara

Rappelle-toi Barbara
Il pleuvait sans cesse sur Brest ce jour-là
Et tu marchais souriante
Épanouie ravie ruisselante
Sous la pluie
Rappelle-toi Barbara
Il pleuvait sans cesse sur Brest
Et je t'ai croisée rue de Siam
Tu souriais
Et moi je souriais de même
Rappelle-toi Barbara
Toi que je ne connaissais pas
Toi qui ne me connaissais pas
Rappelle-toi
Rappelle-toi quand même ce jour-là
N'oublie pas
Un homme sous un porche s'abritait
Et il a crié ton nom
Barbara
Et tu t'es jetée dans ses bras
Rappelle-toi cela Barbara

Barbara

Remember Barbara
It was raining hard in Brest that day
And you were walking with a smile
Beaming splendid streaming
In the rain
Remember Barbara
It was raining hard in Brest
And I passed you on Siam Street
You were smiling
And I smiled too
Remember Barbara
You whom I didn't know
You who didn't know me
Remember
Remember that day anyway
Don't forget
A man was taking cover under an archway
And he cried out your name
Barbara
And you threw yourself into his arms
Remember that Barbara

Et ne m'en veux pas si je te tutoie
Je dis tu à tous ceux que j'aime
Même si je ne les ai vus qu'une seule fois
Je dis tu à tous ceux qui s'aiment
Même si je ne les connais pas
Rappelle-toi Barbara
N'oublie pas
Cette pluie sage et heureuse
Sur ton visage heureux
Sur cette ville heureuse
Cette pluie sur la mer
Sur l'arsenal
Sur le bateau d'Ouessant
Oh Barbara
Quelle connerie la guerre
Qu'es-tu devenue maintenant
Sous cette pluie de fer
De feu d'acier de sang
Et celui qui te serrait dans ses bras
Amoureusement
Est-il mort disparu ou bien encore vivant
Oh Barbara
Il pleut sans cesse sur Brest
Comme il pleuvait avant
Mais ce n'est plus pareil et tout est abîmé
C'est une pluie de deuil terrible et désolée

And don't hold it against me if I speak casually
I speak like that to everyone I love
Even if I've seen them only once
I speak like that to everyone who's in love
Even if I don't know them
Remember Barbara
Don't forget
That wise and happy rain
On your happy face
On that happy city
That rain on the sea
On the arsenal
On the boat to Ushant
Oh Barbara
What a stupid-ass thing war is
What have you become now
In this iron rain
Of fire and steel and blood
And the one who held you in his arms
Lovingly
Is he dead and gone or still alive
Oh Barbara
It's raining hard in Brest
As it rained before
but it's not the same anymore and all is ruined
It's a rain of terrible and desolate grief

Ce n'est même plus l'orage
De fer d'acier de sang
Tout simplement des nuages
Qui crèvent comme des chiens
Des chiens qui disparaissent
Au fil de l'eau sur Brest
Et vont pourrir au loin
Au loin très loin de Brest
Dont il ne reste rien.

From *Paroles* by Jacques Prévert, © Editions Gallimard, 1949.

It's no longer the same storm
Of iron and steel and blood
Just clouds
That die like dogs
Dogs that disappear
In the water falling on Brest
And rot far away
Far far away from Brest
Of which nothing is left.

(Translated by Lisa Neal)

À ★★★

Tu es mon amour depuis tant d'années,
Mon vertige devant tant d'attente,
Que rien ne peut vieillir, froidir ;
Même ce qui attendait notre mort,
Ou lentement sut nous combattre,
Même ce qui nous est étranger,
Et mes éclipses et mes retours.

Fermée comme un volet de buis
Une extrême chance compacte
Est notre chaîne de montagnes,
Notre comprimante splendeur.

Je dis chance, ô ma martelée ;
Chacun de nous peut recevoir
La part de mystère de l'autre
Sans en répandre le secret ;
Et la douleur qui vient d'ailleurs
Trouve enfin sa séparation
Dans la chair de notre unité,
Trouve enfin sa route solaire
Au centre de notre nuée
Qu'elle déchire et recommence.

RENÉ CHAR (1907–1988)

To ★★★

You have been my love for so many years,
My headiness from so much waiting,
That nothing can age or cool;
Even what awaited our death
or slowly managed to fight us,
Even what is foreign to us
Both my eclipses and returns.

Closed like a boxwood shutter,
An extreme and compact chance
Is our chain of mountains,
Our compressed splendor.

I say chance, oh my hammered lover;
Each of us can receive
Part of the mystery of the other
Without divulging its secret;
And the suffering from elsewhere
Finds at last its separation
In the flesh of our unity,
Finds at last its solar path
At the center of our cloud
That it tears and begins anew.

Je dis chance comme je le sens.
Tu as élevé le sommet
Que devra franchir mon attente
Quand demain disparaîtra.

From *A une sérénité crispée*, in *Recherche de la base et du sommet* by René Char, © Editions Gallimard, 1955.

I say chance, as I feel it.
You raised the mountain summit
That my waiting must cross
When tomorrow disappears.

(Translated by Lisa Neal)

PHILIPPE JACCOTTET (1925 . . .)

Aube

Heure où la lune s'embue
à l'approche de la bouche
qui murmure un nom caché

au point qu'on y distingue à peine
le peigne et la chevelure

From *Airs* by Philippe Jaccottet, © Editions Gallimard, 1967.

PHILIPPE JACCOTTET (1925 . . .)

Dawn

A moment when the moon mists over
as a mouth draws near
whispering a hidden name

so that it's hardly possible
to tell the comb from the hair.

(Translated by Lisa Neal)

Bilingual French interest titles from Hippocrene

TREASURY OF FRENCH LOVE POEMS, QUOTATIONS AND PROVERBS
Edited and translated by Richard A. Branyon

This beautiful gift volume contains poems, quotations and proverbs in French with side by side English translation. Includes elections from Baudelaire, Hugo, Rimbaud and others. Also available in audio cassette read by native French speakers and American actors.

128 pages • 5 x 7 • W • $11.95hc • 0-7818-0307-1 • (344)
Audiobook: 0-7818-0359-4 • W • $12.95 • (580)

TREASURY OF CLASSIC FRENCH LOVE SHORT STORIES
In French and English
Edited by Lisa Neal

These 10 short stories span eight centuries of French literature. Nine celebrated French writers are represented: Marie de France, Marguerite de Navarre, Madame de Lafayette, Guy de Maupassant, Rétif de la Bretonne, Alphonse Daudet, Auguste de Villiers de l'Isle, Gabrielle-Sidonie Colette, and Jean Giono. The text includes the original French with side by side English translation.

159 pages • 5 x 7 • 0-7818-0511-2 • W • $11.95hc • (621)

DICTIONARY OF 1,000 FRENCH PROVERBS
Edited by Peter Mertvago

Organized alphabetically by key words, this bilingual reference book is a guide to and information source for a key element of French.

131 pages • 5 x 8 • 0-7818-0400-0 • $11.95pb • (146)

COMPREHENSIVE BILINGUAL DICTIONARY OF FRENCH PROVERBS
Monique Brezin-Rossignol

Francis Bacon once remarked that the genius, wit and spirit of a nation can be discovered in its proverbs. This unique bilingual collection includes 6,000 French proverbs, arranged in alphabetical order in French and English.

400 pages • 5 x 8 • 6,000 entries • 0-7818-0594-5 • $24.95pb • (700)

From Hippocrene's French Library

FRENCH-ENGLISH DICTIONARY OF GASTRONOMIC TERMS
Bernard Luce
20,000 entries • 500 pages • 5½ x 8½ • 0-7818-0555-4 • $24.95pb • (655)

FRENCH-ENGLISH/ENGLISH-FRENCH DICTIONARY & PHRASEBOOK
5,500 entries • 233 pages • 3¾ x 7½ • 0-7818-0856-1 • $11.95pb • (128)

BEGINNER'S FRENCH
Marie-Rose Carré
465 pages • 5½ x 8½ • 0-7818-0863-4 • $14.95pb • (264)

FRENCH-ENGLISH/ENGLISH-FRENCH PRACTICAL DICTIONARY
Rosalind Williams
35,000 entries • 5½ x 8½ • 0-7818-0178-8 • $9.95pb • (199)

HIPPOCRENE CHILDREN'S ILLUSTRATED FRENCH DICTIONARY
• for ages 5 and up
• 500 entries with color pictures
• commonsense pronunciation for each French word
• French-English index
500 entries • 94 pages • 8½ x 11 • 0-7818-0847-2 • $11.95pb • (663)

FRANCE: AN ILLUSTRATED HISTORY
Lisa Neal
214 pages • 5 x 7 • 50 b/w illus./maps • 0-7818-0872-3 • $12.95pb • (340)

PARIS: AN ILLUSTRATED HISTORY
Elaine Mokhtefi
150 pages • 5 x 7 • 50 b/w illus./maps • 0-7818-0838-3 • $12.95pb • (136)

Hippocrene's Bilingual Love Poetry Library

African
0-7818-0483-3 • $11.95hc

Arabic
0-7818-0395-0 • $11.95hc

Czech
0-7818-0571-6 • $11.95hc

Finnish
0-7818-0397-7 • $11.95hc

French
0-7818-0307-1 • $11.95hc

French, Volume 2
0-7818-0930-4 • $11.95hc

German
0-7818-0296-2 • $11.95hc

Hungarian
0-7818-0477-9 • $11.95hc

Indian
0-7818-0670-4 • $11.95hc

Irish
0-7818-0644-5 • $11.95hc

Irish cassettes
0-7818-0748-4 • $12.95

Italian
0-7818-0352-7 • $11.95hc

Italian cassettes
0-7818-0366-7 • $12.95

Jewish
0-7818-0308-X • $11.95hc

Mexican
0-7818-0985-1 • $11.95hc

Polish
0-7818-0297-0 • $11.95hc

Polish
0-7818-0969-X • $11.95hc

Adam Mickiewicz in Polish and English
0-7818-0652-6 • $11.95hc

Roman
0-7818-0309-8 • $11.95hc

Russian
0-7818-0298-9 • $11.95hc

Russian cassettes
0-7818-0364-0 • $12.95

Spanish
0-7818-0358-6 • $11.95hc

Spanish cassettes
0-7818-0365-9 • $12.95

Ukrainian
0-7818-0517-1 • $11.95hc

All prices are subject to change without prior notice. To order **Hippocrene Books**, contact your local bookstore, call (718) 454-2366, visit www.hippocrenebooks.com, or write to: Hippocrene Books, 171 Madison Avenue, New York, NY 10016. Please enclose check or money order adding $5.00 shipping (UPS) for the first book and $.50 for each additional title.